Advance Praise for Bill Bregar, author of "Protect Your Store!"

"If you're experiencing theft in your store and are ready to take action, I highly recommend you get in contact with Bill. He and his team have helped us tackle our theft issues by installing a system at all entrance and exit doors throughout our store. He even came to our store and trained our staff on how to point out and handle shoplifters. This book is only going to enhance our efforts even more."

- Tina Lee, *Owner, Vice President of DeWayne's*

"Having attended Bill's seminars for retailers and subsequently having him train my staff onsite, I was thrilled to see his wisdom compiled into this necessary read! Bill delivers his years of loss prevention expertise in a must-read for any retailer, as well as your management team. We will be incorporating his shoplifting policy and procedure segment into our manual first thing tomorrow! Reading this book could very well be the best thing you do for your business all year!"

- Margaret Hamm, Owner of Monograms Plus of Cullman, LLC

Protect Your Store!

Protect Your Store!

*The Shoplifting Prevention Guide
For Small To Medium Retailers*

Bill Bregar

ISBN: 197391252X
ISBN-13: 978-1973912521

DEDICATION

I want to dedicate this book to my awesome wife Conny Bregar. We married in 1980 and I would wager to say that Conny never expected our lives to turn out the way that they have. She has always been an inspiration to me. Always supporting and encouraging me and offering me constructive criticism and advice. A better partner in life and business I could not have. The writing of this book was no different. A value could never be placed on her ideas, editing and suggestions. Conny's rock solid support, pushing me to be the best made this possible. Thanks my love.

Protect Your Store!

CONTENTS

ACKNOWLEDGMENTS

I want to thank all the retailers I have worked with over many years. I can only write a book like this because of the many years I have been helping people solve theft problems with their stores. I feel so privileged to help you and your stores become more profitable by reducing loss, which should not happen, but sadly does.

I have written many hundreds of blogs, magazine articles and the like in my career. But this was my first attempt at a book. The idea for this book was first proposed by my Marketing Guru and friend Ron McDaniel at Buzzoodle. The Marketing field is full of charlatans that talk the talk but can't do the walk. Ron is a true web marketing expert that actually gets the job done spectacularly. His endless ideas and strategies have pushed Loss Prevention Systems forward in many ways. Once we started this book project, Ron has been there every step of the way. With a watchful eye, suggesting ideas, changes and concepts that I would have missed. A few times he had to hit me in the head with a stick rather than "suggest". I am forever grateful for his marketing leadership and drive.

I have also found that Editors are more important than I have ever imagined. Behind the scenes they really clarify and refine ideas and concepts, many that start as words that are a bit rough. I am fortunate to have Neo McDaniel, of Buzzoodle (and Ron's clearly better half) on the team as Editor. Neo has refined concepts to make them even clearer for you to read and understand.

FOREWORD

By James Learmonth
Loss Prevention Program Manager,
Whole Earth Provision Co. Austin, Texas.

The modern retail environment is without question, a challenging place to do business successfully. With the arrival of the internet retail model, modern brick and mortar retailers face competition that didn't exist just a few years ago, eroding market share and pressuring margins more than ever before. To have success in this environment, a modern retailer must not only flawlessly execute every detail in their business model, they must totally capitalize on the primary advantage they hold over their online competition. That advantage is presence. The traditional retail model allows a potential customer to contact and experience merchandise in a way that an online retailer will never be able to duplicate. The Internet retailer attempts to compensate for the lack of interaction by trying to lure customers with lower prices and satisfaction guarantees, in exchange for not being able to create contact between the customer and the merchandise.

One of the ways an online retailer is able to create price advantage is through lower overhead and business efficiency. Slimmer staffing requirements, warehouse vs. retail space rent advantages, and even drop ship models all contribute to operational efficiencies not available to a retailer operating an actual storefront model. At the end of the day, however, all else being equal, a customer will almost always choose to have an interaction with merchandise prior to purchase, with perhaps the exception of consumable goods of known quality. The storefront retailer must both maximize the customer experience with the product, and prioritize any available business efficiencies in order to keep the price gap as small as possible, and the interaction experience as important as possible to the consumer.

One of those business efficiencies is called loss prevention, or inventory control, or asset protection, or any of numerous other fancy names. Large scale retailers have recognized the need for loss prevention as integral to their business for decades. If you have read this far, you are likely a smaller retail (say, under $50 million/year) operation that is frustrated because you know you are losing money to theft, fraud, and any number of other criminal activities taking little bites out of your business every single day. Loss Prevention is an intimidating step to take for a smaller retailer, because it costs money, and you're not sure if it will pay off, and who has time to learn to do all that stuff anyway? Whether your business is a one store shop, or a $100 million per year specialty retail chain, I can guarantee you that making fundamental LP concepts part of your operation will absolutely pay off.

I first met Bill Bregar after I entered my position as "LP program manager" of a ten location retail chain doing about $50 million per year in revenue. I used quotes because there was no program, only a collection of guesses and attempts to prevent loss by folks in the company whose area of expertise was retail, and NOT Loss Prevention. So, a decent size company, but one that hadn't been ready to take the plunge until inventory shrink reached truly painful levels. If this sounds like it could be you, don't wait. Get started ASAP. Every day you wait equals more of your dollars leaving in the hands of thieves. As a former cop myself, as well as a business analyst, I had a great background for this task, but I also needed help. I began making cold calls to various LP solution providers, and of everyone I talked to, (most didn't even call me back) Bill was the only one who was ready, willing, and even excited, to help me with MY business problems. My company's transformation in loss performance is a testament to Bill's expertise. The Math doesn't lie.

One of the most important concepts Bill explains is that as a business operator, inventory and subsequent revenue shrink due to various criminal activities is a business problem to be managed, and NOT necessarily crimes to be solved. Fundamentally, business problems are just math problems. Solving crimes and putting criminals in jail is Police work. Now, understand that doing those things does nothing to help your bottom line; there's no money in doing police work. However, transforming your business into the type of target that criminals choose to avoid, and keeping those problems out of your store(s) has a huge positive impact on your bottom line, and makes all of your business calculations (math problems) turn out better. Of course, it's always satisfying to catch bad guys, and help them get their punishments for their misdeeds, but it's not always the best business decision to do so. Information Bill provides here is crucial to understanding the true impact of crime on your business, (hint: it's much worse than you thought, and worse than your accountant says it is.) which in turn is invaluable to helping you make the best decisions in the interests of your business. Bill also discusses the critical concept of risk vs reward in the context of Loss Prevention operations.

In this book, Bill brings to the table his decades of expertise in Loss Prevention, and presents it to the reader in an easy to understand, and more importantly, easily scalable format so that it is useful no matter the size of your retail operation. He offers guidance and information that is immediately useful, and relevant to almost every small to medium size retail business operator. In the event you are starting from scratch, as I did, consider LP literacy as sort of a two stage process. I recommend reading it twice. Once with an eye to help clearly understand the impact of the problem on your business, and the potential for improvement. Then, make your own calculations using the formulas Bill provides with numbers from your own situation. These results can also be used effectively later if needed, to justify your requests for infrastructure funding, and payroll expenses for training. Then, once the real impact of the problem is better understood, I recommend you reread it again to absorb the guidance and recommendations on how best to prioritize and address the issues that are causing your business the most pain. If you've recognized a need for Loss Prevention in your business, but aren't sure what to do, take the first step, and read Bill's book. Remember, your competition in online retail doesn't really worry about retail theft. Anything that you can do to close that efficiency gap, and press your advantage as a brick and mortar "touch and feel' retailer is something you should take full advantage of. Once again, the Math doesn't lie, and Bill's proof is in my results.

In less than 18 months, my company transformed LP performance from the bottom third of retail shrink performers, to the top 10 percent. We achieved ROI on our LP capital expenditures in less than 12 months. If you will go ahead and also plug your data into those numbers, the results speak for themselves. How can you decide not to move forward?

Protect Your Store!

ABOUT THE AUTHOR AND INTRODUCTION

Shoplifters are the bane of retailer's existence. Competition in the retail jungle is tough enough without losses. I can quote many studies and figures giving you the billions of dollars lost due to shoplifters, but you do not really care about that. The fact is that they steal from YOU! And you want to fix the problem in your store. You have little to no control what happens in the rest of the retail world, you can only fix issues in your store.

The goal of this book then, is to help you fix YOUR shoplifting problem in your store. To do this, I want to give you real tools that you can put to work immediately or with little effort. If you are looking for additional solutions, those can take more time and more investment, but we do have them.

The Author working as Police Officer with one of the more colorful characters in the Colorado Mountains

My journey in this has been extensive. I started out in life wanting nothing more than to be a police officer. That was my goal. After a number of violent experiences, and the realization that I was only responding to incidents rather than predicting them and thus preventing them, I found myself in the Loss Prevention field. Frankly, I wanted more in my career.

So, I went into the loss prevention trenches. Starting with the apprehension of shoplifters as a store investigator all the way to director of loss prevention for several major retailers. Along the way, I have caught more shoplifters than I care to remember. I have interviewed and interrogated over 2,300 employees for theft, wrote policy and procedure, and developed loss prevention programs for many retailers. With the encouragement of my awesome wife, Conny, I started Loss Prevention Systems, Inc. (LPSI.) Now, after two decades and with thousands of retail clients, I have had the pleasure to advise and work with retailers in many verticals and sizes to stop losses before they occur.

Over the years, I have run into some pretty weird situations with shoplifters. Part of preventing shoplifting involves apprehending the thieves who are stealing. In one situation, I apprehended a guy who had stolen a framed picture of Christ. He did not fight me, resist, run or anything else that we were always prepared to deal with. But, when the Police arrived at the store and we were switching handcuffs on the shoplifter, he turned to me and said, "This is not a very Christian thing you are doing to me". This guy STEALS and I am the sinner!

Another time, I stopped and detained a middle-aged woman for stealing about $300 worth of new tennis shoes. I had personally witnessed her switching tags to lower priced shoes. She had a fairly heavy Eastern European accent. Again, while police officers were taking her into custody, she stated that I was discriminating against her because she was European. The police officers taking her into custody, whom I knew very well started laughing. She looked at them with shock when they told her, "Lady this store is owned by a French company and he (pointing to me) is married to a German citizen (I met my clearly better half, when I was in the Army stationed in Germany). Then, they reminded her that she had the right to remain silent and that they would prefer that she exercise that right.

Bill Bregar in Washington DC on a GRA trip to discuss Georgia retail concerns with GA House and Senate members.

Another all-time favorite is the guy who stole a $1.00 fishing lure from a sporting goods store. That was all he took! I stopped him and took him into custody. When I got him back to the security office, I emptied his pockets (he was handcuffed) and was bagging it up for the police when I discovered a "wad" of cash well over one hundred dollars. I was shocked (still naive then) and asked him why he stole a minor $1.00 item when he clearly had the cash to pay for it. He said, "I wanted to see if I could get away with it". I just shook my head and told him that it was good that he had the cash on him, as he would need it towards bail.

I have found over the years that you can prevent shoplifting and be entertained at the same time.

My experience also landed me on the board of directors for the Georgia Retail Association. For 11 years, two of those years as chairman of the board, I was guiding retailers in the state of Georgia not only in the loss prevention world, but steering the federal and state legislative agenda and goals that supported all retailers in the state.

Having spent many years in the retail world and having gained lots of knowledge and experience, I now want to convey an easy to follow roadmap addressing your shoplifting problems. I have broken this book into short chapters, each addressing the problems you are most likely experiencing. But do not short change yourself. It is critical that you have an understanding of the overall shoplifting problem and other solutions that may not apply right now, but that you will likely experience sometime in the future. And again, always keep in mind that in an effort to prevent loss, we must be proactive.

Protect Your Store!

CHAPTER 1
WHAT AM I REALLY LOSING TO THEFT AND
HOW DO WE ATTACK?

The thing that amazes me the most about retail loss, is that some retailers really do not understand how much they are actually losing. Many folks I have spoken with over the years think that when a shoplifter, or even an employee steals, let's say, $100 dollars worth of merchandise, cash, supplies, etc…that the $100 is all they lost. NO, it is not. The loss is much greater than that.

Consider this: if your net margin is 2% (for every dollar you sell you profit 2 cents) then that $100 loss is going to cost you $5,000 in additional sales to break even (100/.02=5,000). So, after all your expenses have been paid, including rent, payroll, insurance, utilities, merchandise cost, and then something for you, you are clearing 2 percent. In some retail verticals such as grocery, the margin is even less. For other retail verticals the margin is more. In your particular case, your margin may be different, but you simply need to change the percent and recalculate to see where you fall.

That $5,000 in sales is simply to break even, not to make a profit. You have to make up for the loss. There is absolutely NO WAY to sell through this. You cannot fix inventory shrinkage (shrink) or losses with sales. Believing otherwise is deluding yourself. So get that issue straight in your mind and business philosophy first. A number of very reputable, thorough studies conducted throughout the years, all say about the same thing.

The breakdown of retail loss on an annual basis is roughly like this:

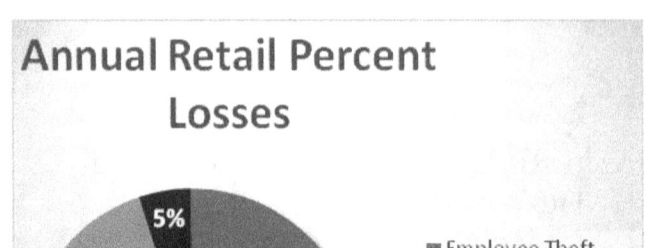

Again, this changes from year to year but the ratio stays somewhat the same. Of course, employee theft is an alarming percentage, but in this book we are focusing on the 35% of your losses due to shoplifting.

So, let's say your losses in a fiscal year due to shoplifting is $20k. At the 2% margin, you will have to make an additional $1,000,000 in sales, simply to break even. With shoplifters, you do not lose all that at once. In the retail jungle, shoplifters are biting pieces off of you one small nibble at a time. $5 here $200 there. Our response then should take you into the weeds and grass on the jungle floor.

How much more merchandise are you going to have to purchase, ship, stock and ultimately sell to stay afloat, let alone break even? The reality is, that you cannot answer that question because there is no answer. You would be out of business.

Now, keep in mind that on average an individual shoplifter steals $550 per incident! It does not take too many incidents like that to wipe you out.

Our approach has to be to go on the attack, NOT defense. Defending yourself only telegraphs to the predators in the jungle that you are weak and vulnerable.

I have never realized that so many small retailers are actually afraid to take proactive measures to prevent shoplifting in their stores. As a Loss Prevention professional, who has apprehended more shoplifters than I care to remember, I have a difficult time with this fear. I can assure you that shoplifters will sense your fear and you WILL become one of their favorites. It's like blood in the water to a shark.

A proactive approach sends the message "leave me alone, I am not afraid of you". To prevent shoplifting, you must not be afraid to provide great customer service. That is the foundation to a successful store and a profitable year. Wow…this is something you strive to achieve anyway.

Great customer service drives your good customers into the store and drives the shoplifters out the door, down the street into your less prepared competitor.

Technology is also critical. It provides you with 24/7 security coverage on your merchandise. It never takes a day off or calls in sick. So, when your floor coverage is low, you are still protected. A well-lighted, clean, and neat store also tells shoplifters that you are on the ball and know where your merchandise is and account for it.

Also, you must call the police whenever you catch a shoplifter regardless of age, sex or any other factor. If you do not, the smell of blood will be in the water. If the shoplifter knows that the worst they face is harsh words from you or your staff, then so what! Remember, most states have merchant laws in place that protect you from both civil and criminal action. You just have to follow some simple rules. I will show you where to look for your States laws later in this book.

You and your staff need to be trained in how to deal with a shoplifter when you do make the decision to apprehend. But, more importantly you need to practice it before you do it in real life. You can do this by role playing in store meetings or training sessions.

It is simple logic. The shoplifter will take the path of least resistance. Make their path in your retail business an uphill climb strewn with boulders, vines and traps. They will go away!

In the retail industry there are TWO solutions to shoplifting. Yes, you read that correctly, there are only two solutions to shoplifting and you have to combine them to fix the problem, otherwise, you are just fooling yourself. It is kind of like keeping the dangerous animals in the real jungle at a distance with a fire. They are still there, ready to pounce when the opportunity presents itself and you are not looking. You and your staff cannot spend your entire time focusing on shoplifters. You have to run the store and make sales.

The two solutions for shoplifting are training and an Electronic Article Surveillance System (EAS) such as a Sensormatic system. Training should find its basis in your store policies that have been defined.

So, with that said, let's get some items out of the way right away. Yes, Loss Prevention Systems, Inc. (LPSI) sells Sensormatic systems nationwide. Yes, I have a vested interest in that. No, this book is not a sales pitch. I am going to refer to Sensormatic systems in later chapters because, well, those are the systems I know and fully understand. Another main reason is that Sensormatic is actually a leader in this field and always has been. Many of the top retailers world-wide use Sensormatic systems. But enough said about that.

One solution will not be successful without the other. Your understanding of your individual shoplifting problem through training and your policies will only take you so far. The EAS system is there to back you up, and you WILL need backup. You and your staff cannot be everywhere at once and watch everyone. Shoplifters create distractions or take advantage of exactly those situations to steal.

Likewise, the Sensormatic system is not effective at all without Loss Prevention training. It is not just how to apply or remove tags and labels. Of course, your staff needs to be trained on which merchandise to tag, how to apply the label, hard tag, bottle cap, Keeper, and how to remove or deactivate it at the Point of Sale (POS). But, training is also about how to detect, observe, approach and dissuade the shoplifter. Think of the fire you have going in your camp in the jungle. The predators are afraid of the fire (you and your staff). They are not going to get close enough to get burned but they are lurking out there on the edge of darkness, waiting. But waiting gets old when you are hungry (for the merchandise). So they will try to distract you to one side of the fire so they can sneak in behind you. That is where the EAS system comes into play. Even if they do steal, they will be detected and deterred.

CHAPTER 2
WHO IS STEALING FROM YOU?

We know that one of every ten people who walk into your store is there to steal. YES, that includes YOUR store. So, you may be thinking to yourself "well, I don't think that applies to me". Then, why are you reading this? You have suspected that you have a problem for some time and your suspicions have been confirmed by empty packages you find on the sales floor, inventory results, customers telling you what they saw and the shoplifters you have caught.

What is the old saying that the first step in recovery is to admit you have a problem? The great news is that we are going to attack this as what it is, a business problem. You will have the tools to solve it just like you solve any other business problem. For example, if you are a grocer and one of your freezers starts making noise, are you going to wait until it fails and lose thousands of dollars in frozen merchandise, or are you going to call for service before the failure? So, let's first understand the creatures that are in our retail jungle.

I can think up a lot of names for the creatures who are stealing from you. Slime, low life and many others that are not very nice to say. But there are three groups of shoplifters: Impulse, Amateur and Professional.

The largest group by far is made up of the Impulse shoplifters. An Impulse shoplifter is just that. They will only steal, if the conditions are just right. Almost half of your shoplifters are Impulse shoplifters. **Impulse shoplifters** steal usually to keep the merchandise for themselves. The great news about this is that they are the easiest to stop. Impulse shoplifters are dissuaded by an EAS or Sensormatic type system. But more importantly, studies have shown that most Impulse shoplifters will not steal during the current visit to your store if they are GREETED. Wow, think about that. All you have to do is say something like "Welcome to my store" with good eye contact, and like magic, the Impulse shoplifter will probably not steal from you during THAT visit. Why? Because they have been noticed and recognized.

Amateur Shoplifters steal to keep the merchandise, but they may also give it to their friends. Their intent when they enter the store is to steal, and they probably know what item they want. Like the Impulse shoplifter, the Sensormatic system will deter them. They may know a bit more about the  tags and labels, but that knowledge also brings fear to that particular kind of shoplifter. They also understand that we have some very sophisticated tags and labels. Some they know, and some are hidden and not evident. So that also works in our favor.

Professional shoplifters who enter your store are there for one thing only, and that is to steal as much as they can get. They usually select items that have a good resale value. The merchandise they steal from you is sold sometimes back to the same vendor or distributor that sells to you. Professional shoplifters only make a small margin on what they steal, so volume is critical.

There are not as many Professional shoplifters as the news media would lead us to believe. It makes a nice story every Christmas, but I believe the vast bulk of shoplifting losses to my customers are from the Impulse and Amateur shoplifters.

Get rid of any preconceived image of a shoplifter that you may have. Shoplifters can be and are going to look just like your real customers. They do this in part to blend in. They do not want you to single them out because of the way they dress, groom, etc. They want to blend in. That is the camouflage these type of shoplifters use in the retail jungle.

Now here is a scary part. Like I mentioned before, one in ten people that walk through your door is either an impulse, amateur or professional shoplifter. They may even be a person that you see often. If they can successfully steal from you over and over, why not come back over and over? They see you as the unskilled, uneducated merchant. Now, here is the even scarier news than that. Shoplifters talk to each other. Just like you and your friends, shoplifters hang around with… well, other shoplifters. Just like you hang around with friends that are in many ways like yourself. Word has gotten around in the jungle that you are an easy target. It's time to feast on YOUR merchandise.

Protect Your Store!

CHAPTER 3

THE ATTACK ON SHOPLIFTING: WHAT WORKS AND WHAT DOESN'T

As I said before, there are two and only two ways to attack shoplifting economically. To be successful you must have a thorough understanding of both. These two methods are training and an Electronic Article Surveillance System (EAS) such as a Sensormatic system. In the retail jungle BOTH must be used and implemented simultaneously.

Training includes not just how to react to a shoplifter that has already stolen, but more importantly how to attack. Like the jungle, predators only respect and fear real force. A sign that says "Shoplifters will be prosecuted" or other such nonsense, are worthless and quite frankly a waste of signage. That space can be better served by directing legitimate customers towards a sale item. Shoplifters know that you could and even would put them in jail. But even knowing this they will steal anyway. Why? Because if your strategy is to display a sign to prevent shoplifting, they know you really do not know what you are doing.

Both you and your staff have to be trained and practice what you learned. The really great news is that the concepts for shoplifting prevention always include great customer service which will increase your sales.

EAS or Sensormatic systems must be designed and implemented properly. A poorly designed or cheap system will not only be a waste of your capital, but will set your program back because the system will become an annoyance to your staff and your customers resulting in it being shut down. So, now you have an inoperable system, wasted the money, and are missing a full fifty percent of your shoplifting program.

I will discuss both Training and EAS in greater detail in later chapters. But what I want to tell you now, are about the things that don't work. To make it easy, I will list them. The list is long, so I will focus on the things I see most often.

Signs - I discussed this earlier. But, I will add something else here. We have a hard time getting people to look at our marketing signs in the store to begin with, so what makes you think shoplifters will even care about a sign that promises certain death for shoplifting? The truth is, they don't.

I also feel that it cheapens your store appearance to your customers. Use that precious space for something that counts, like a sale or holiday special. Most of our Sensormatic system antennas have built in Ad Signage panels. This allows you to greet the customer with a "welcome," let them know about a sale item, or whatever you want. But, I think it sets the wrong tone for the other 9 out of 10 legitimate shoppers that walk in your door to see something that is a negative as soon as they walk in your door.

Mirrors - This was great stuff 30 years ago. But again they have little value mainly because you cannot see enough detail. Like signs, I think they can trash up the appearance of your store. You are trying to create a retail shopping experience not make people feel like they are visiting their distant black sheep cousin in a Federal Prison.

Closed Circuit Television (CCTV) - This tool has some value but it is after the fact. Shoplifters know that you do not have the payroll dollars to have someone spend their time watching live.

One of the only industries that can do this are the casinos.

Four to six cameras watch one dealer by security folks who understand exactly how theft at the gaming table occurs. You do not have that kind of skill or time. In addition to this, it is really not cost effective to have enough cameras to effectively cover even a small store footprint. CCTV is reactive not proactive. That said, you still want a CCTV system covering key points such as the Point Of Sale (POS) and the entrance and exits. However, set your expectations correctly. This is a reactive system. In other words, we are going to use it to figure out exactly what happened as it pertains to a given incident like, descriptions, direction of travel, evidence for the police, etc.

One thing that drives me crazy about CCTV systems is the angle the cameras are looking. Great shot of the top of his head. Maybe he should try one of the hair loss products you carry and get a new barber. But, what we really want to see is the shoplifter's face. There are great cameras that go on your doors' frame. They blend in, and it is unlikely that anyone would even notice them. That camera can be placed at about 4.5 feet off the floor and it gets a great face shot as the person exits.

Display Cables - I see limited benefit to a cable system that ties down display items such as power tools, phones, tablets, cameras, etc. We want the customer to pick up the item and feel its weight, grip, and feel, but if the old style cables are a tangled mess, it will cause frustration to your customers and staff.

Modern display management systems have moved us out of the dark ages. In our retail jungle, we can even have very high dollar merchandise out and displayed. These new units have retractable cables, built in tamper alarms and more. They also enhance the look of your display merchandise and send a clear signal that you are professional and serious about your merchandise presentation and security.

Store Investigators - Been there, done that. A fully trained and experienced store investigator is an awesome asset and can have a serious impact on shoplifting. The problem is that most retailers except the big box stores cannot effectively afford and deploy them. Even with the payroll budget the big box stores have for this, it is rare that there are always store investigators on duty. On top of this, the civil and criminal laws are ever changing. This requires guidance of senior loss prevention management and a corporate attorney. Small to medium size retailers simply cannot manage this type of asset.

Small or Large Caliber Handguns, Explosives and Poison - Don't even go there as tempting as it may be!

Always remember, solving a shoplifting problem is no different from any other business problem. Research the solutions, find someone you trust, implement the solution and follow up to ensure it stays fixed.

CHAPTER 4

TRAINING: START WITH POLICY AND PROCEDURE

Even if you are a one store operation, you need to have a shoplifting policy and procedure in place. This is not as complicated as you are thinking it will be. Below is draft wording of the beginning of a shoplifting policy and procedure

Definition:
Store management is responsible for preventing losses due to shoplifting and when preventive efforts fail, to apprehend known shoplifters. It is a policy requirement that only those persons who are directly observed shoplifting (stealing merchandise, cash, or any properties of the company). Will be detained and turned over to local law enforcement agencies for prosecution. The detention of a suspected shoplifter will only take place after all of the criteria that will establish intent to steal, as well as the state and local shoplifting statutes, have been satisfied.

Procedure:

I. General Information
Management personnel are the only associates authorized to detain a suspected shoplifter. Management may detain individuals only when they are certain that the suspect has shoplifted from the store.

Detention should not be based solely on statements made by non-associates. While we are extremely concerned with shoplifters and the losses they cause; we are equally concerned with our reputation and our customers. Remember one extremely important fact--we would rather have a suspected shoplifter leave the store than to detain an innocent customer. A lawsuit resulting from an improper apprehension is not only very expensive, but also extremely damaging to our reputation.

II.   Detention Procedures

Prior to detaining a suspected shoplifter, there are several observation requirements which first must absolutely be met. These observation requirements are for the protection of the company, the suspect being detained, and you. Under no circumstances will suspects be detained other than by the prescribed procedure listed below.

A.   Observation

1.   The subject must be personally observed by an associate while removing/concealing merchandise from a counter, display rack or shelf. If a suspect is seen concealing an identifiable piece of merchandise without first being observed picking up the merchandise, then an apprehension is not justified. Management must be absolutely certain the suspected shoplifters still have the concealed merchandise on their persons or in their belongings/possessions when they attempt to exit the store.

2.   Do not let the suspect out of your sight, even momentarily, from the time the shoplifting occurs to the time the shoplifter attempts to exit the store. There is always the possibility that the suspect will change his mind or may intentionally dispose of the merchandise, thereby baiting for a false arrest.

3.   Be certain you have knowledge of the merchandise, can identify it, and can tell where it has been concealed.

4.   Additional evidence of intent is established when the suspected shoplifter has passed beyond the point of no return (lease line) with the merchandise concealed.

5.   Policy requires the suspect be detained at or just beyond the exit door.

B.   Detention

1.   Only when all of the above criteria have been met is management permitted to detain a suspect for shoplifting the known article.

2.   Do not touch the suspects. Detain them by saying, "Just a moment sir/ma'am". Be confident, self-assured, and speak with authority,

but most importantly, be polite. Treat the suspects as you would like to be treated if you were in their place.

Remember that the great majority of shoplifters we have contact with are not hardened criminals, but children, housewives, office workers, etc.

3.   Do not accuse the suspect of shoplifting. As you detain an individual, identify yourself by stating, "I am an employee of the store, I believe you may have forgotten to do something". If you have followed these procedures, you will be able to advise the suspect what and where the merchandise in question is. At this point politely state, "Will you please come to the office with me?"

4.   When detaining a suspect, attempt to have a second associate with you. This will provide you with a witness and a psychological deterrent to resistance or violence.

5.   If the suspect offers resistance or refuses to return to the store, terminate the attempt. Do not use force. Do not chase shoplifters. The safety of our associates and customers is a priority.

6.   When escorting suspects to the office/stockroom, walk directly behind them and watch their hands. This is when an attempt might be made to dispose of the merchandise.

C.   Interview
1.   Do not enter the office/stockroom without a witness present. This is extremely important when our associate and the suspect are of the opposite sexes.

2.   If you have followed the guidelines, you will be able to ask the suspect to produce the merchandise in question. You may request, "Would you please place all merchandise for which you have not paid on the desk?"

3.   You must inform the suspect of the reason for being detained.

4.   Should the subject ask to use the telephone, the request is to be granted only on short local calls.

5.   Suspects will never be questioned against their will. You may ask, "Would you mind showing me what you have in your purse/pocket/bag?" If a suspect refuses, DO NOT press the matter. Instead, call the police.

6. Under no circumstances are physical searches of shoplifters to be conducted. All shoplifters are to be carefully watched during the detention to prevent dangerous situations from developing. If you feel your safety is in danger have another associate call the police before you enter the office/stockroom.

7. Call the police immediately. One of the questions frequently asked by defense attorneys is "Was the suspect aware that the police were called?"

8. Request identification from the suspect, retain it and give it to the police upon their arrival.

9. Never leave the suspect alone. Stay in the office until the police arrive.

10. Have a witness present at all times. This will help prevent the suspect from attempting to run away.

11. When the police arrive, they may require store management to retain the evidence. Place the merchandise in question in a bag in the officer's presence. Put the name of the suspect, the date, item listing of all merchandise including price, and your initials on the outside of the bag. Then staple the bag closed and have the police officer sign his name and the date. Following these steps will preserve the chain of evidence.

12. If you cannot follow these guidelines due to a violent, resistant, and uncooperative suspect, immediately call the police.

13. After a police report has been made, immediately call Senior Management

III. Reasons for Following Detention Procedures
A. If followed; these guidelines will give us a substantial case for a successful court prosecution.

B. These guidelines will limit our liability in a lawsuit, as most state laws, if adhered to, provide protection for the retailer.

C. We will not be exposed to illegal or improper apprehension litigation or the consequences thereof.

D. Intent is the most difficult thing, which we must prove, and following these procedures will assist in establishing that very important factor.

E.   If followed closely; we will not expose the company, its associates, or you to a loss of reputation in making poor detention.

Note: Remember, most of the shoplifters we apprehend are not career criminals. It is imperative that suspects be treated with respect and courtesy, as you would desire to be treated if you were in their place.

This is just a start. Each company has different ways of looking at how they want to operate. The policy should tell you and your staff how to react to and deal with suspected or known shoplifters. Loss Prevention Systems provides this and other LP related policies and procedures to our customers. You can modify them to fit your needs. If you would like a copy of this policy in Word format, contact me via email at bbregar@losspreventionsystems.com and put "shoplifting policy" in subject line. No, you do not have to buy anything. I am happy to send it to you.

We must also keep in mind the laws at federal, state and local levels. For the most part, all states have some form of "Merchant Law" on the books that allow you to stop a shoplifter without fear of civil or criminal repercussions. Again this varies by State.

So, "Why do I need to do this?" Well, if you engage with a shoplifter on any level and the situation becomes either a civil or criminal case, it is likely that a court will ask you why you did what you did. Having that documented and following it generally impresses the court, a jury and the opposing attorney.

Now you need to begin teaching your staff and yourself how you want to approach the shoplifting problem. Remember, shoplifters come in three types: impulse, amateur and professional. The really great news is that the same techniques work on all three types with the exception of Organized Retail Crime (ORC) which is another type of professional.

Impulse shoplifters steal when the opportunity presents itself and usually keep the merchandise for themselves.

Amateur shoplifters tend to steal consistently, in most cases keep the merchandise but will also give it away to friends or family.

Professional shoplifters steal consistently, because this is how they earn a living. Your merchandise is sometimes sold to the distributor that you buy your goods from. They only earn a small amount on the dollar that they steal, so quantity is important. This means they have to work fast. Most of the time they are stealing to "fill an order". If the person they are selling your stolen merchandise to needs a certain type of name brand or style purse, a specific cordless drill, cell phone etc, that's what they will steal.

A new term for some professional shoplifters has come into the retail jungle. They are referred to as organized retail crime (ORC). Many times this is related to gang activity. They can be violent. In many cases, the adult hierarchy uses juveniles for the actual theft because these kids are usually released quickly by authorities, often within hours and are back out on the street shoplifting again the same day.

An ORC gang may hit a store with 15 people or more, overwhelming the store's staff. They simply grab arm loads of merchandise and run out the door. Employees and customers have been injured and worse.

Planning for these kinds of situations and training employees on what to do will improve their safety and security.

CHAPTER 5

TRAINING YOUR STAFF AND UNDERSTANDING SHOPLIFTERS

So, how do we proceed from here? To train yourself and your staff to stop shoplifters you need to look at what makes them tick. Shoplifters are human beings. Although from a retailer and law abiding citizen point of view, they are a lesser life form. To understand how they think, we need to look inside ourselves. We have all done things that we should not have. Took a grape off the fruit counter and ate it, or took a dollar out of mom's purse. But, as we mature, we understand that this is not the way we wish to live our lives. In fact, we grow up to be law-abiding Americans. In other words, we grew up. Shoplifters are nothing more than thieves (that did not grow up). The reasons they steal are not important. The important reason is the way they think. So, look back at yourself.

I will use myself as an example. I remember that I was in a convenience store and stole a pack of sunflower seeds. I was probably in sixth or seventh grade. I will never forget how I felt. I looked around from side to side. I was nervous and scared. I am quite sure that I looked suspicious. So, I put the package in my pocket. What I did not see was the manager watching me behind my back. The manager ended up calling my father. I would have really preferred that he would have called the police. At least, my life would not have been in danger with the police!

We have all been there in some form. Remember that feeling? Think about it. You are scared, you know you are committing a crime, and you are doing something wrong. It does not matter how cool you act on the outside, it is what is happening on the inside that counts. That fear and nervousness are the tools we are going to use as a weapon. Shoplifters are nervous and react to even the slight feeling that they may have been discovered.

In our goal to prevent shoplifting loss, we have to keep in mind that juveniles pose a different set of challenges. Unlike an adult, kids steal for different reasons. Of course, they have the usual reasons; like wanting the item, needing the money etc, but kids though, have another reason: peer pressure.

You will not fully prevent shoplifting loss by juveniles unless you understand the peer pressure that may be driving them. We, as adults, would not even consider jeopardizing our freedom, reputation and risk criminal and civil sanctions because someone dares us to shoplift. We are probably not going to shoplift in order to steal something for a "friend".

Why do juveniles do this? I have been told that our brains do not fully develop, and our morals and ethics do not begin to become a permanent part of us until we are around twenty-one years old. After that we are less likely to be swayed by someone because of the desire to fit in. Think about it. You may have started smoking at that time because "your friends did it" or because of your desire to fit in. This is a reason why we give juveniles special status in our country. They are not held to the same legal status as an adult. In many states, a juvenile's criminal records are sealed to protect them.

Kids tend to travel in groups of two or more when involved in this type of activity. They deserve special attention when in your store. Of course, this does not mean that every kid in your store is there to steal. But kids without adult attention and supervision should be watched.

The good news is that in most cases you can generally prevent shoplifting of this type easier than adults. Good eye contact and customer service skills will for the most part stop the individual kid from stealing on that visit. However, let them get away with it and you will become the magnet for juvenile shoplifters. We know how fast word will travel with kids. There are no secrets with them since knowledge is power.

More than 60% of shoplifters steal from the same store because they got away with it; the first time and subsequent to that, the store culture made them feel comfortable. It makes sense. If we create an environment that makes the shoplifter relaxed enough to continue, they will also tell their friends. Your store is or will become a magnet to shoplifters.

Once caught, very few shoplifters will return to the same store to make another attempt. The key is to first deter them. If that does not work, make them feel uncomfortable once they do pick up an item and attempt to conceal it, or better yet, catch them.

However, habitual shoplifters, after being apprehended, will return to the same store when no Electronic Article Surveillance (EAS) system is in place because the chance of being caught a second time is only 2%. Shoplifters want your merchandise, either to keep or sell it. The goal is to make them uncomfortable enough or shut them down completely. This will send them down the street to another retailer who is not proactive. That reputation will also spread among shoplifters.

When do shoplifters steal from you? The answer is whenever YOU give them the opportunity. Yes, if you create a shopper friendly, shoplifter hostile environment, then shoplifters will go elsewhere. They will probably go to your retailer neighbor or competitor who is not protecting themselves. Shoplifters look for times when the staff to customer ratio is out of balance. Busy evenings, Saturday mornings or anytime they know you are not paying attention. This includes right at opening when you are still getting cash into the drawer, cleaning up (which should have been done the night before), or being focused on your coffee. The same issues apply at closing time. Everyone is focused on going home, especially if that closing is on a Friday or Saturday evening. Everyone wants to get home, or go see their friends, and that's when shortcuts are taken. Attention is not where it should have been.

Shoplifters look for these particular times, and they share this information with other shoplifters, both orally and online. They talk about the best and easiest places to steal. And they talk about the how, what and when to steal. If your store becomes known to shoplifters as an easy target, then you will be one of their places of choice.

What about age? Shoplifters can be any age. Age alone should never be a factor in detecting shoplifters. I have caught shoplifters of all ages.

What about race? Again, if you use race as a factor you are misguided. Shoplifters come from all races, colors and religious backgrounds. Do not fool yourself into thinking that one group of people steal more than another. In fact, we can easily find stories of anyone from movie stars to attorneys who shoplift. I once caught a district court clerk from a court that sees a huge volume of shoplifting cases. Shoplifters can be anyone.

So, what do shoplifters look like in the retail jungle? They look like YOUR NORMAL CUSTOMER. That is their camouflage. They want to blend in. Of course, there will be exceptions. However, the homeless, drug user look that you may have stereotyped in your mind could be a shoplifter, but not for the reasons you think. There are a lot of really good people that are down on their luck in life who would never even think to steal.

Now, we need to ask ourselves what is the mindset of a shoplifter predator and how do we use that to attack and chase them away from our section of the jungle?

Shoplifters think differently than other people. They have not just an intent to steal, but the mindset to do so. They associate with others that are just like themselves. To better explain that, think about your friends, the people you hang out with on a personal basis. What are they like? Probably a lot like yourself. We tend to socialize with people who share similar feelings, traits, political views, religious views, work ethics, education or intellect levels. That is a reason in my mind that we each gravitate to certain clubs, churches, gangs, associations and more. It is because we want to be with others like ourselves and who we feel good around.

Shoplifters are no different. They hang out with other shoplifters or people who share that desire. They compare stories, experiences, best places to steal, when to steal and more. That is comfortable to them. They conspire on justifications with each other. "It's a big company with too much money, they will never miss it," "They treated me ___ (insert some made up or real injustice here)___ , or some other reason. The fact is, we as retailers do not care what the reason is. What we want to do is use that knowledge to understand how to detect them. Shoplifters are predators that feed on your merchandise.

Watch for these indicators when observing customers that could be shoplifters:

Quick or sudden head movements or turns

Are they watching you or your staff, or are they paying attention to the merchandise?

Are they carrying a large bag, purse or backpack?

What do they have in their hands or in their shopping cart? Is it all expensive or frequently shoplifted merchandise? Are they headed towards a more concealed area of the store with that merchandise?

Is the clothing they are wearing appropriate for the season? Wearing a winter coat in the Summer is an example.

Protect Your Store!

CHAPTER 6

HOW DO SHOPLIFTERS STEAL FROM YOU?

Concealment - First and foremost shoplifters steal by putting your merchandise into their pockets. It's easy, a natural motion and virtually everyone has pockets. Merchandise can also be placed under their clothing or even a child's clothing who is with them.

Next in popularity are purses, shoulder bags and backpacks. They provide an easy way to conceal larger items and a much larger volume of merchandise. The question that arises is whether you have any reference in your store policy regarding these items being allowed into your store? Of course, it is unlikely that you will stop purses from coming into the store. But, if that "purse" is the size of a Samsonite overnight bag, then we may want to address that issue. Many retailers have policies that do not allow personal items like these into their stores, or at least they try to limit them.

Next on the list is a shopping bag from another retailer. In malls and strip centers this is an issue. It is not practical and probably not good for business if you stop this type of traffic. This will cause legitimate customers from coming in. However, if this is a huge issue for your store, you can look at checking bags in to be stored behind the cash/wrap while the customer shops. This is a nice benefit and can be spun that way to your customers. Storing their bags for them allows them to shop your store much easier. The down side is that you end up taking responsibility for their property. If a loss (real or made up) or damage occurs, you end up in an undesirable position.

Infant strollers are another big concern from my point of view. They are akin to a shoplifter bringing in a covered wagon (minus the horses) into your store. Modern strollers have pockets, and enclosures for everything; from a month's worth of diapers to a cooler built into them that can be lined to make an EAS system less effective. Infant strollers are great shoplifting wagons. On top of this, I have seen shoplifters take a piece of merchandise and put it under the child. Because no one is going to yank the kid out of the seat to check.

Another issue is switching merchandise packaging. It is taking merchandise that they want and is higher priced and putting it into a box of less expensive merchandise. Think perfumes, tools, just about anything that is in an unsecured box.

Price tag switching is pretty much a thing of the past because of the use of barcodes. But a shoplifter could purchase an item from your store, take that item home, recreate the barcode (free software for this), create a sticker with the less expensive barcode on it and then place that sticker over the barcode on a higher priced item in your store.

In a similar method, they can take merchandise they want to steal and put it inside a larger merchandise box or packaging. As an example, think about purchasing a mailbox. They can be very large and they come inside a cardboard box. Many other merchandise items will fit in there.

Keep an eye on your fitting rooms, if you have them. Criminals know that they're one of the few places in the store where you won't have surveillance. So, limit the number of items a person is allowed to bring in and post a fitting room attendant whenever possible. Be aware of your high-risk merchandise. Usually particular brand names, trendy styles or items tend to grab a shoplifter's attention. Make sure that you are also aware of the trends, and pay close attention to the location and accessibility of those items. You should be proactive and stay one step ahead in order to prevent shoplifting in your establishment.

Fitting rooms, like in the restrooms, are places where criminals know there will be no surveillance. So, be mindful of any individuals attempting to take merchandise into the restrooms with them. Lastly, instruct your associates to greet each and every customer with a warm and open demeanor. Ask if they need assistance and let them know they will be nearby if any questions or concerns arise. I call this the "kill 'em with kindness" method. Any legitimate customers get terrific customer service while any would-be thief is made aware of your constant and watchful eye.

Refunding merchandise that was never purchased is another issue. Of course, we know that a shoplifter can steal a piece of merchandise from you and then later return to the store and ask for a refund claiming they lost their receipt. My solution to that is that receipts should always be required.

But, there is another twist on this in the retail jungle. The thief removes the tag from new merchandise, claims it was purchased, and receives the cash. And they NEVER LEAVE YOUR STORE.

One way I have found that shuts down refund fraud by shoplifters is to not only require a receipt, but to require official photo ID. Shoplifters do not want you to know who they are. When you do this, ensure that your staff understands that they must actually look at the ID including the photo, and compare it to the person standing in front of them. An Asian male standing there with the ID of a Latin female might just be a little suspicious.

One time, I was in one of the stores where I worked as a Regional Loss Prevention Manager. I had just finished up an internal investigation and was in the store manager's office finishing my paperwork. Linda, the manager, came into her office and mentioned that they had a suspicious customer/return at the service counter. I asked her if I could handle it and she said to go for it. This retailer is a very large building materials, hardware retailer. So, I proceeded to the service counter. The man was trying to return a bath faucet valued at $70. I identified myself as a "manager" (not Loss Prevention) and asked if I could help him. He said he wanted to return a faucet set and did not have a receipt. I told him no problem. I took the faucet off the counter so he could not just scoop it up and go off. Besides, I told him no problem, at least at that point. This started exercising control over the situation.

I looked the faucet up on the computer. It showed that we had two in inventory for the last six months (not a fast mover)! And a quick check showed that one was missing with no sales during that period. I told him I just needed his ID and I got out a return slip to start filling out. Well, he stood there with a frozen look on his face and after an unpleasant silence where I said nothing but continued to smile and look at him he said, "My ID is out in my truck". I said no problem I will wait for you. I waited 45 minutes. Okay, I really didn't wait that long but it felt like it. The guys in the lumber yard said they saw him drive off.

Think about it. Would you abandon a legitimately purchased $70 item just because your ID was out in your truck? Of course not. He was a thief who stole the item. I do not know if he stole it that day, the previous day, or during another shopping trip. It does not matter. Taking control of the situation, asking for ID and clearly making it known that his information was going to be recorded shut him down.

Another technique for suspicious returns is to accept the return, record the customer's information and inform them that after you can research it you will send them a check. Chances are you will never hear from that person again. If you do then let them know you cannot find a record of that sale and ask again for the receipt and more details.

Here are some other points you should consider and train your staff on with regard to refunds:

Watch for individual customers that make frequent refunds. Your POS system should be able to track this.

Watch for the same person using different names and addresses to obtain refunds.

Look at the receipt to see if it is a "used receipt"? This would be a receipt from a previous purchase that is used to obtain a refund on additional merchandise. Again, they pick it up in the store and walk up to get a refund.

Shoplifters can create a counterfeit receipt on a PC using a real one from your store. Many times staff can spot these because of errors including format, dates, spelling and SKU number errors.

Distraction is another method that thieving shoplifters use. They work with a friend and create any kind of distraction. I have seen faked injuries, children screaming, "customers" who get angry at staff and more. This draws your staff's attention away to that area while the other one shoplifts. When I was a police officer, I was trained to look at who was going the other direction when I was responding to a call. The suspects were usually going the opposite direction I was. You and your staff need to do the same thing. First, not everyone needs to run over to the scene no matter how juicy it is. Second, while dealing with the situation at hand keep an eye on your surroundings.

Shoplifters ask to see more secured merchandise than employees can keep track of, thus ensuring an easy way for them to pocket it.

Another method is using another person or a small child to keep the employee occupied while a partner steals merchandise. We are Retailers, not babysitters.

Then there is shuffling merchandise around and just creating confusion in general.

Professional shoplifters use "booster" clothing or devices. For example, a booster box is a box that could appear to be gift wrapped, or is a merchandise box that has been rigged with a trap door in it. The professional shoplifter sets the box on top of the merchandise they want to steal and it disappears inside. Shopping bags and any other item can be rigged that way.

Booster clothing are garments that a shoplifter makes and then wears into your store. They look like regular clothing.

For example, a coat could be easily modified by cutting the inside liner to allow your merchandise to be slipped inside. A woman can wear booster "bloomers" under a loose-fitting skirt. A slit is cut into the skirt to look like a pocket opening with a corresponding slit in the bloomers. The bloomers end above the knee and are tied off. Merchandise is then able to be dropped into the bloomers and it slides down along her leg.

One of my Store Investigators once caught a woman with six cordless drills and batteries hidden this way. He said she kind of "clanked" when she walked. But you could not tell she had them on her.

These professional merchandise predators will use unique and innovative ways to steal. Again, their goal is volume. And like the jungle, if you are an easy target, they will descend on you in a pack and feast.

CHAPTER 7

TRAINING YOUR STAFF

This book is not meant to replace the training that we provide. There are many details that I simply cannot layout here. Loss Prevention Systems, Inc. (LPSI) provides training for the detection and prevention of shoplifting, employee theft, pre-employment interviewing and vendor fraud free of charge to our customers (enough of that commercial.) However, you should create an environment in your store where shoplifting is routinely discussed and training is brushed up on frequently.

I feel you should start your group training discussions with issues that happened within your own store. For example, was an empty merchandise package found hidden somewhere in the store? That should be discussed at a quick weekly meeting or daily "huddle". Ask your people for input and ideas on how to stop or solve the issue at hand. You will be pleasantly surprised when you ask for their thoughts. They may know more about those issues and solutions than you or they think. Are you hearing any stories from your retail neighbors? All of these details should be discussed along with solutions that work for your store.

The following is an outline that you can use to discuss shoplifting with your people. You could concentrate on one bullet point a week or whatever works for your situation and time allotments.

DETERRENTS TO SHOPLIFTING

The primary solution to reducing shoplifting is: CUSTOMER SERVICE

Employees can help deter shoplifting by keeping their eyes open. Alert, keen, well-trained employees become the most important deterrent to shoplifting.

All customers must be greeted upon entering the store. Acknowledge them by pleasantly stating, "I'll be with you in a moment."

Watch all customers in a pleasant, courteous and interested manner. Let customers know that you see them even if you are busy.

Serve each customer promptly. Good customer service is always pleasing to the honest customer--but shoplifters hate it!

Remember, by providing good customer service you are removing the opportunity for a shoplifter to steal.

The store should be adequately covered at all times by store employees. This can be accomplished by the following:

Zone coverage. Divide your sales floor up by sections and have a staff member responsible for that area.
Movement of employees to handle multiple customers.
Constant surveillance of suspicious groups entering the store.
Customers are not allowed inside the confines of the checkout.

Customers are not allowed in the stockroom.

If you suspect a customer is being tempted to pilfer, be courteous while carefully and openly watching that person. Approach the customer and ask if assistance is needed. Remember, good customer service will deter most shoplifters.

Make periodic "security ghost calls" over the PA system such as:

"Security to section ___ ". Make up a section/isle location. For example, if your store uses isle numbers, then use a letter in the call.

Service a suspected or known shoplifter "to death". Stay with them. You could even pick up a clipboard and act as if you are looking at stock. As they move around, you follow.

Known shoplifters can be overtly followed. Every time they pick up a piece of merchandise approach them and ask them if they need help.

If you see a customer conceal merchandise, pleasantly ask one of the following:

"May I help you?"

"Can I show you a _____ to go with (concealed item)"?

"Can I hold (concealed item) for you at the register?"

"Will this be a charge or cash sale?"

"May I ring this purchase for you?"

If the customer does not respond by replacing or paying for the item, and you are positive merchandise was taken and concealed, you may be dealing with an actual shoplifter.

At checkout EVERY CUSTOMER should be asked, "Is there anything else?". There are 2 very good reasons for this question: 1) Legitimate customers may remember an item they forgot. 2) Impulse and amateur shoplifters may feel anxious or guilty about what they have done, they may fear that you know or saw them, and produce the concealed item.

Empty boxes or packages may indicate that a shoplifter is in the store.

All employees are expected to know the correct merchandise pricing policies.

Cashiers should be alert to altered or switched SKU and price tickets. If the price is questionable, perform a price check.

Cashiers should open containers such as cartons, unsealed boxes, etc.

Cashiers must ensure that customers do not rearrange items on the counter. Shoplifters may try to mix items already rung with other merchandise.

Protect Your Store!

Cashiers must make sure all purchases are bagged. The sales receipt must be placed inside the bag or handed to the customer.

CHAPTER 8

ELECTRONIC ARTICLE SURVEILLANCE AND SENSORMATIC SYSTEMS

So, you have your staff trained up. They understand the value of customer service in shoplifting prevention. But, the retail jungle is a very dangerous place. These thieves come at you from all directions and with ever changing methods. The

big problem is that you and your staff are really there to sell and make money for the company. That is the real goal.

The shoplifting scourge can be a time consuming business by reducing not only your sales, but putting a drain on your manpower resources. These predators look for and create opportunities that are favorable to them.

So, if your staff is busy with customers, stocking, special projects or one of the other thousands of things you need to get accomplished, what do you do? You cannot allow the shoplifter to dictate YOUR business. That is playing defense. We need to stay on offence against shoplifters, gain the high ground and keep it.

By doing this, you create an atmosphere where good customers feel welcome and special, but the shoplifters quickly learn they are in hostile territory and simply leave.

This is where Electronic Article Surveillance (EAS) or a Sensormatic system comes in. Again, I am going to say up front that throughout this book I am going to refer to Sensormatic systems when talking about EAS. Part of the reason for this, is that Sensormatic has some of the most advanced systems in the market. There is more to them than the sound beeping and the light flashing. Like all other technologies, EAS has progressed. Sensormatic has driven many of these innovations.

There are two technologies for EAS. Radio Frequency (RF) and Acousto-Magnetic (AM).

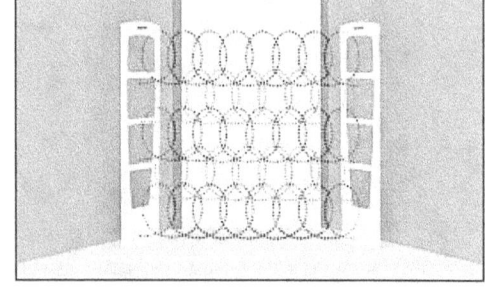

The hard tags and labels for both RF and AM operate in much the same way. The system's antennas at the doorways are looking for the hard tags or labels. The antennas create an electronic field if the tag or label enters the system and sees it. That causes an alarm. Those tags and labels are not battery powered. They are inert.

RF involves exactly that, a Radio Frequency. These systems are tuned from 8-0 to 9.5 MHz's. Nothing else is allowed on those frequencies by the FCC. Many times, shoplifters and good customers that trip the system may claim that something else they have on them is setting the system off. That is highly unlikely. There are other reasons a system will set the alarm which we call "phantoms", but I will discuss that later in the book. A person could claim that an access system card, their cell phone, hearing aid, pace maker, car keys, etc., is causing the alarm. The most probable cause is that they have a tag or label on them. It could be one from your store or another retailer.

Acousto-Magnetic or AM systems work on an entirely different technology. Some of the advantages of AM systems are that they have significantly less false alarms and this technology allows for wider isle widths. Another advantage is that Sensormatic systems can detect AM labels and tags on merchandise items that have a significant amount of metal. RF systems are at a significant disadvantage when it comes to placing a label on any merchandise that has metal or in some cases electronic circuitry.

AM has also been around for some time. And if copying something is a form of flattery, then AM has achieved that flattery. Sensormatic has driven the innovations in the AM market, so again Sensormatic being the leader that it is, has been "flattered" many times.

You have probably heard of Radio Frequency Identification (RFID). RFID is taking the standard RF label and putting it on steroids. An RF system will detect an RF label, but it cannot tell one RF label from another RF label. RFID labels are individualized. If you have RFID labels on say five thousand bottles of aspirin, the system can tell which bottle is number 2183. Of course, this opens up a whole new world. Inventory can be taken by an RFID system and we can tell where aspirin bottle number 2183 is located in the store. We also know when it leaves the inventory (sold). The RFID system can manage inventory levels and trigger reorder. The list is endless. However, this is not a cure-all just yet. Merging an RFID system with your accounting system is a daunting task. You would have to label each and every item in your store.

But that is the future. Sensormatic already has antenna sets that we install every day that have the ability to be upgraded to include RFID.

The key benefit of an EAS system is that it represents the backup to your customer service efforts. What I have learned over the years is that you have to have both for your program to be successful.

Protect Your Store!

CHAPTER 9

SYSTEM CONCEPT, DESIGN AND PURCHASING A SENSORMATIC EAS TYPE SYSTEM

Systems come in two basic forms. A single door (3') or double door (6') application. For wider applications such as a mall entrance, additional antennas would be added to cover the entire space. Floor systems and overhead systems are available.

Floor systems consist of a specialized encased antenna that is buried in the floor, usually under concrete. The electronics on the other hand, are housed in a remote cabinet.

Overhead systems involve another type of specialized antenna that is mounted over the entryway area. Depending on the hard tag or label to be used, the detection distance is a factor that needs to be considered.

The system you choose is installed by a Technician. He/she bolts it to the floor, wires it, and then programs the system to meet your needs. You and your staff apply tags and labels to your merchandise and you are in business.

The systems work for you in a number of ways. First the actual physical presence of the system tells shoplifters that you are protected and to go away. Shoplifters and some customers know what those antennas at the doorway are for.

I have had some retailers tell me over the years that they are concerned what kind of message is being sent to their good customers by having a system installed and in plain view. The reality is that good customers really do not care. They are not thinking about theft, they're shopping. Think about what we discussed earlier in the book. Shoplifters think differently than good customers. I think you should find it interesting, if someone is "concerned" about your system. What we have found out is that when a system is installed, there are some "customers" that get upset. Ask yourself why. The security has absolutely no impact on a good customer. The people who get angry are the people that have been stealing from you all along. They are used to and dependent on you keeping the status quo. So now you have just taken that opportunity away from them.

You can label and tag every piece of merchandise in your store, but that is probably not necessary. We want to protect about 20% of the merchandise that is causing 80% of your problems. In some cases, you may want to protect more, but the 80/20 rule is a good standard to use initially. If what you need to protect is clothing or anything with fabric, then you should lean towards hard tags. A hard tag is made up of two pieces; the tag and the pin. The pin goes through the fabric and into the back of the hard tag. It can only be removed with a special detacher or key. Labels are applied to any other merchandise.

Sensormatic labels are very thin and have an adhesive. Labels like hard tags are active 24/7. But hard tags are removed at the Point of Sale (POS) by staff. Labels are "deactivated" at the cash/wrap by staff when the merchandise is sold. The label is "killed" by the deactivator and simply goes out with the customer on the packaging. It is disposed off by the customer with the packaging. Most likely the customer does not even know it is there in the first place.

Labels and hard tags should be manufactured by a reputable source such as Sensormatic.

Cheap hard tags can be pried apart with a tool such as a knife or screwdriver. If the clutch that holds the pin is poorly made, then it is easy for the shoplifter to remove it.

Labels are even more critical. Cheap labels are exactly what you get. I have seen instances where 50% of the labels on a roll did not even work. The adhesive on some labels are so poor that the adhesive dries up quickly, and the label can be peeled off or simply falls off the merchandise. Labels with good quality adhesive set up and after 30 minutes will not come off. Another problem with cheap labels is that you deactivate or kill it at the POS, and by the time the customer reaches the exit, the label has reactivated itself and now you get an alarm.

When a legitimate customer picks up an item and approaches your cash/wrap to purchase it, your staff will ring the item up and at the same time remove the Sensormatic protection. If the merchandise is protected by a Sensormatic label, they will pass the label on the Sensormatic Deactivation pad. Deactivation "kills" the label. The label cannot be reused. The exceptions to this fact are non-Sensormatic brand labels. We have seen self-reactivation by cheap labels occurring. After the label is deactivated, it goes out with the merchandise and packaging to be discarded by the customer; it should never reactivate itself and set off the system.

For hard tags on clothing, or cloth material type merchandise, your cashier removes the hard tag and pins it with a special detacher or key. The hard tag and pin are then reused over and over.

If a shoplifter on the prowl picks up a protected item and attempts to remove it from the store, the Sensormatic systems' antennas at the doorway go into a visual and audible alarm alerting your staff. It would be nice if Sensormatic Systems would give us options for nets falling from the ceiling (just like for animals in the jungle) and explosive hard tags, but so far, I just cannot seem to get Sensormatic Senior Management interested in that idea.

Oh well, I will keep trying for you! (Just kidding people!)

Designing the overall system for your retail store is normally pretty straight-forward. We look at the doorway and consider the environment around it. Your merchandise offerings, problem merchandise, frequently stolen items, store design and look, as well as your budget. Those are the main parts of the equation. Certain models of systems perform better in some environments than others. You may want features such as people counting, direct access to the system for viewing alarms, customer count and more.

Something that I think retailers often overlook is the use of the system for other purposes. As I mentioned above, some Sensormatic systems have the ability to count customer traffic. This is different than traffic through the Point of Sale (POS). Do you know what percentage of customer traffic you are converting to sales? Do you have enough staff on, or do you have too many folks on at certain times? If  there is not enough traffic, is your store open earlier than it should be? Should you be closing later? We can even count traffic in particular areas of the store. Does that end cap display draw enough attention? What times of the day are customers shopping in certain areas? These are the types of questions that customer counting can answer.

Customer counting reports show this data by the hour and day of the week. They come to you automatically every week. You can get a finished report or raw data that you can merge into your sales data.

Another major feature is the use of AD Panels. Some Sensormatic systems have built in AD Panels. This allows you to greet customers, promote a sale or special, or simply put your brand or logo up. You could also charge your vendors or suppliers for advertising space. Many times, a vendor will give you advertising dollars to promote their items over another brand. The beauty of Sensormatic AD Panels is that you can simply change them out yourself in a matter of seconds. You or your printer can design the poster, print it, or switch it out daily if you want. Keep in mind that this is the first thing your customer sees when they walk in. On top of that, it is not taking up any more floor space. You are using the antennas for additional revenue producing duties. AD Panels also help to blend the system into your store looks for your good customers. The shoplifting predators still recognize what they are.

Your stores' electronic environment is another big consideration. There are factors that can cause problems for a system in some retail environments: We always want to keep items like ice machines, freezers, ATM's, lottery machines, etc. at least four feet away from any Sensormatic antenna. They can cause interference that could trigger false alarms. If possible, it is best to keep that kind of equipment off of the same electrical circuit (breaker) for the same reasons. Sensormatic systems require a standard 110 volt electrical circuit or in some cases a 220 volt circuit. But in most cases your standard outlets near one of the antennas usually works well.

You also want to keep fixture design in mind. For obvious reasons, you cannot have any tagged merchandise within four feet of the system. If you must have merchandise close to the system because of space considerations, you need to display only the items that are not tagged. This could be large bulky items or items that are not easily stolen.

Shopping carts, hand basket racks, railing and other metal can also cause a problem and may need to be moved away from the antennas. Pay attention to the condition of your doors. If they look and sound like they are about to fall off the hinges, they could also cause interference. Many times, a bit of maintenance is all that is needed to get doors in acceptable shape.

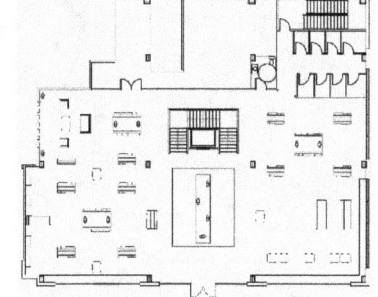

When we install any floor mounted system, we have to run a cable between the two antennas. Normally this cable goes inside a floor mounted wire mold that is meant to be walked on. It is commercial grade and made of steel. A much cleaner way to do this is to have the cable placed under the floor. If you are on a concrete slab, then we trench the concrete about 1.5 inches down by 0.25 wide. The cable is placed inside that trench and then covered with concrete filler. The cable disappears under the floor. Your floor covering, such as tile, or carpet can go right over. Many times, the most practical way to do this is during construction or remodel.

There are systems that do not mount on the floor. Sensormatic has systems that mount on the door frame or inside the door frame. They have a very clean look. The wiring and electronics can be mounted out of the way or above the ceiling tiles.

The deactivation chassis and pad are installed at your POS. The chassis is often mounted in the cash/wrap somewhere. The deactivation pad which is about one foot square is mounted on the underside of your countertop, near the POS. As long as there is no metal in the counter top then the pad will deactivate or kill labels right through the countertop. Store countertops can decrease the distance for a label to be deactivated but normally they work pretty well.

If you use scanners built into the cash/wrap like a grocery store, the deactivation "pad" is normally installed as part of the scanner. The beauty of this is that the deactivation system will only kill a label after it has been scanned. Many new scanners have the deactivation loop built in from the factory. We simply attach the deactivation chassis to the port provided on the scanner.

The deactivation system can also be used to detect the presence of a hard tag. That helps keep customer alarms down by warning the cashier to remove the hard tag.

When purchasing a Sensormatic system you should first look at the model that will fit best your stores' appearance. It could be a floor mount, door frame mount, overhead, below floor system, clear acrylic or wood. But always keep in mind that you want two antennas on a standard system. This creates a much better detection field. After taking into account those considerations, narrow your choices down by your budget. It's pretty simple: more bells and whistles equal higher cost. But keep in mind that the Return On Investment (ROI) for most Sensormatic systems is about 5.5 months. That means that at about month 6 you are putting money back on the bottom line.

The Installation of an average set of antennas at a doorway takes only about four hours. You should factor in that there may be a return trip or two by the Technician to adjust the system. This is normal. This is commercial grade equipment and is meant to stand up to the retail jungle.

I always suggest that you do not overkill on the purchase of tags and labels. Try smaller quantities of different styles to see what works best for you. You should always consider having a variety of labels and tags that work for specific merchandise. Kind of like not putting a square peg in a round hole.

Protect Your Store!

CHAPTER 10

DEPLOYING A SENSORMATIC SYSTEM

The Sensormatic system, in itself, is a known deterrent to theft. A few normal customers may have a vague idea what the system antennas are for, but most have no clue what they are or how they work. On the other hand, shoplifters know what they are, and are fearful of them. The system tells shoplifters that you are protected, that you have thought through your shoplifting situation, and that you have paid attention to the problem. But, you cannot stop there. Thieves will test you and your system time, and time again. If they find that the system is off or not working, then the jungle feast is on.

Your staff must be knowledgeable and make full use of the system. Many times, we as business owners or managers, believe we have found a solution to fight the shoplifting in our store by purchasing and deploying a Sensormatic system. We then pat ourselves on the back believing we have fixed our problem, only to find that six months later, we have the same problem again.

I guess some of this is natural. We deal with so many and such a diverse amount of issues on a daily basis, that we believed we have fixed a problem and move on. But shoplifting cannot be treated that way. Unless you stay on the offense and continue to improve and refine your defensive and offensive game, you will be the one at the bottom of the retail jungle food chain.

Make sure the system works EVERY day prior to opening. Do this using a test tag or even just a piece of protected merchandise. This task should be assigned to an employee who then makes a log entry verifying the system was tested and functioning. This is no different from any other operational task. You need to follow up on this to ensure that it is not just being logged without testing. If the system is malfunctioning, then get it fixed right away.

Most states acknowledge EAS systems legally as an inventory control system. An alarm on a Sensormatic system is enough to give a retailer a "reasonable belief" that a loss of merchandise could be occurring. This then gives you probable cause to investigate and stop someone. And this is exactly what you want to do. DO NOT just wave them through. The system went off for a reason when that person went through it. Find out WHY!

CHAPTER 11

WHAT MERCHANDISE SHOULD I PROTECT?

To approach the answer to this question you should look at the obvious first. What empty merchandise packaging are you finding? Shoplifters tend to discard packaging and labels before they conceal the object of their desire. Many times they stash these behind other merchandise on shelves, dressing room mirrors, trash receptacles or any other hidden space.

You and your staff know your store better than anyone else, so watch these areas. Any empty packaging should be brought to your attention and a log should be created. Many times, when you see this on paper, a pattern will appear. Record the day of the week, time of day, location and more. This gives you a clear indication that this merchandise should be protected with a label or a tag.

Of course, look at your inventory (you do take inventory, right)? Where is your shrink coming from? In between inventories you should conduct cycle counts on your problem merchandise. It is a simple task to take one or several SKU's and do a daily, every other day or weekly count. You can compare those SKU's to sales and replenish those items. Protect these items as well, if necessary.

Overall, you should look at protecting about twenty percent of your merchandise that is causing around eighty percent of your shrinkage. High end and expensive items should be protected regardless. But keep in mind that low cost items or items that you may not expect, could be causing you substantial loss.

I have a customer that had a trend of losing a lower cost canvas type shoe when shoplifters would leave more expensive shoes alone. The reason for that was professional shoplifters were able to resell these branded shoes easily and quickly, turning a substantial profit.

Some merchandise such as high-end jeans may require double protection. They should have a hard tag in plain sight and a label concealed in a back pocket, just in case. This gives you inexpensive protection for an expensive item.

Speaking of evaluating which merchandise to protect-you should really use a loss calculator when considering what to protect and what not to protect. Like any other business loss, it is kind of like a thermostat. How much heat can you stand before you turn it on? To calculate your ACTUAL LOSS, use this simple formula:

For our example, we will use a stolen item of $200, and a profit margin of 2%. This 2% (or whatever your number is) is what you make after expenses, rent, utilities, payroll, etc., in the end you have a 2% profit margin. So, we take $200 divided by .02 and that equals $10,000. Yes, that is right, you will have to sell another $10K to BREAK EVEN on a loss of $200. No one can sustain that. Your investment in training, policy and procedure, and a Sensormatic system is minor compared to the return on investment.

You can use your Sensormatic Security Systems for more than shoplifting prevention! But in addition to being an anti-shoplifting tool, you can get even more out of them. Consider the following:

Employee theft is also an important issue. Merchandise with Sensormatic tags and labels can also be a deterrent to employee theft as long as you control who has access to detachers or deactivation. This is where the key lock on the detacher also comes in handy. Deactivation that is tied into your POS so that an item can only be deactivated after the item is scanned, will also be a deterrent. Most companies only allow employees to enter and exit from one door. If that door is protected with antennas, then this closes off another way merchandise can be removed.

Another use of Sensormatic tags and labels, is to tag items that you do not want leaving the store. Restroom keys, manager keys, even documents can be labeled. If you have items that sometimes go home with an employee such as a set of keys, the tag can be a reminder. It is not an issue of theft, but if the item leaves, it can create a nightmare for others.

How about tools or other store use items? A hard tag with a flex string or lanyard will help remind someone that they have it in their possession, and to put it back before they go home. What about an employee who is working on a display and is using store tools? He leaves for a little bit and does not secure the tools. A customer then decides he wants that cordless drill or battery for himself.

What about store use items such as calculators or flashlights? A Sensormatic tag or Sensormatic label will solve that. Don't forget other critical items such as pricing guns and the gun that puts the hangtags on clothing.

Protect Your Store!

CHAPTER 12

APPLYING SENSORMATIC LABELS AND HARD TAGS

Label application – Labels come in various sizes. Sensormatic labels can be white, black or have a fake barcode.

Black is most commonly used on liquor, wine, or any product with dark packaging if you want the label to be less obvious.

The barcode also helps to disguise the label.

Recent studies have shown that this visual deterrent is often more effective than just a hidden label alone.

The adhesive on a label is critical. Poor quality adhesives will dry out and allow the label to be peeled off easily and in many case simply fall off after a short period of time. A good quality adhesive will set after 30 minutes or so, and not be able to be removed easily for the life of the packaging.

Label placement is important. Labels should be hidden or placed where it is unlikely the shoplifter will find it. However, the reverse is true with a Sensormatic label that has a fake barcode. Placing it in plain sight may be a form of hiding it in the open.

A best practice is to locate the labels in the vicinity of the manufacture's barcode. This allows your cashiers to easily locate and deactivate the label. With some high value or often stolen merchandise, you may wish to consider protecting it with two labels in different places. Here are a few more recommended dos and don'ts for AM labels:

Label Dos:

Apply the label as close to the product's barcode as possible.

Ensure that the label is applied smoothly and evenly.

Store labels at room temperature (to protect the adhesive) in a secure area.

Label Don'ts:

Cover important or legally required information about the product with the label

Bend or crease the label.

Place an EAS label on food items, unless it is a designated food label.

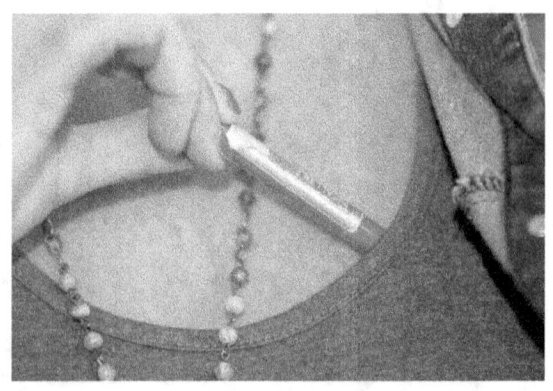

Hard Tags – Like labels, hard tags come in many sizes, colors and qualities. A good hard tag has a strong plastic shell along with a clutch that accepts the pin. These components are welded together. Cheap hard tags

do not generally have good construction, and in many cases, they can be pried apart with a knife or screwdriver.

You should always use a swivel head pin for your normal merchandise. This type of pin resists tampering by a shoplifter. The head rotates or "swivels" in the pin itself. Pins do come in other types. Some have longer pins to allow for thicker merchandise. There are conical head pins that are very difficult for a shoplifter to tamper with using a tool.

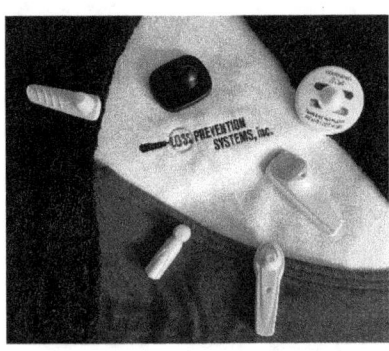

Some hard tags have a raised ring around the pin hole. This raised ring allows the pin to settle down inside it. By doing this, it is much more difficult for a shoplifter to work a tool under the pin head without significant difficulty and damage to the merchandise. Your staff must use the correct pin for the merchandise they are tagging. Too long of a pin, or the pin not being seated fully, gives the thief more opportunity with your merchandise. Training your staff on the differences of pins and how to apply them is critical.

Where you choose to place the tag is also important. Not just from a security standpoint, but also from a selling's point of view. You do not want to place a hard tag on a garment that makes it difficult or even impossible for a legitimate customer to try the merchandise on or be able to evaluate it.

For example, a shirt should be tagged on the back side on a collar seam. This way, the tag is out of the way, will not interfere with the customer trying the shirt on, and will not be a visual deterrent to the customer's decision whether they like the shirt or not.

Another example is trying to use a hard tag on a shoe. Placing the pin through an eyelet may keep the customer from lacing it up and will affect the customer's experience.

You should also be consistent with your placement of hard tags. Remember, the majority of customers visiting your store are good folks. We want to deliver a great retail experience to them. We do not want them to get all the way through the POS, and then have an alarm go off at the exit because the cashier missed a hard tag.

Hard Tag Dos:

Tag in a consistent position on all like garments

Tag in line with your company policy

Tag in a visible position for maximum deterrence

Gently ease the pin through the fabric

Perform the tug test to ensure the pin/tag is locked into position

Store tags and pins/lanyards separately on removal

Ensure bottle tags are positioned on the narrowest part of the bottle neck

Hard Tag Don'ts:

Pierce leather, suede or waterproof materials

Tag in a position that will interfere with the customer trying a garment on

Use bent pins or damaged lanyards

Leave pins on the point of sale area or on the floor

Store tags next to deactivation equipment

Place customer payment cards next to the magnetic detacher

Place multiple tags on one item

CHAPTER 13

WHAT DO WE DO WHEN A SENSORMATIC SYSTEM ALARM OCCURS?

The way your employees respond to the alarm activation system can determine how effective your system will be. A proper response can keep your employees safe and keep merchandise in the building. These are my tips for properly responding when clothing security tags cause an alarm activation.

DO:

When responding to an Electronic Article Surveillance Alarm, suggest that there may be something the person may have "forgotten" to pay for. By giving the person an out, they may be more likely to give the item back. You get the merchandise back and have established that your employees DO respond to alarms.

Respond immediately. When a customer has to wait, they become agitated or walk out. Agitated customers are more difficult to work with and those that walk out provide no opportunity to recover merchandise.

Be polite. Assuming someone has stolen something and being terse or accusatory will probably cause a defensive response, even if the person did not do anything dishonest or illegal. A smile goes a long way in disarming a grouch.

Ask if you can assist in determining what may have caused the alarm activation. Provide possible solutions: Did the cashier overlook something? Did you purchase something at another store that may be causing the alarm? Would you mind if I looked at your receipt to see if any Sensormatic tags were not removed? When you give suggestions to the customer, you give them "outs" without being belligerent. Many times, someone who is trying to steal will be willing to give up merchandise, if they have an excuse made for them.

Do ask to look at a receipt and check inside a bag, purse or backpack. If the patron refuses, you can go back to giving some "outs". Suggesting an error may have been made at the POS, removes fault from the shopper, and are more willing to allow the search .

If merchandise is found that was not paid for, DO treat it as an oversight and Do offer to have the item rung at a register. The customer may "choose" not to purchase the item after all.

If there were Sensormatic tags not removed and it was the fault of the cashier, be sure to apologize for the inconvenience and follow up with the cashier so they are aware of the oversight.

DON'T:

Accuse someone of trying to steal. Depending on the jurisdiction, concealment may not be enough to say someone is shoplifting and that leads to other issues.

Don't try to physically detain someone. The culprit may have a weapon, or they may be violent. You can file a police report after they leave the store.

Don't chase. You endanger yourself and potentially other customers.
Special note about "Incoming" alarms.
Sometimes when a customer walks in to your store, the system will alarm.

Ask the customer:

"Have you purchased something in another store with a system like this?" Other retailers may not have properly deactivated a label that was placed on the merchandise.

"Are you returning an item for exchange or refund?" Was the item they are returning, purchased or stolen?

"Is there any reason you can think of for our inventory control system to alarm?" Let the customer offer input as to why the system is alarming. They may become nervous and give you more information.

In some cases, shoplifters will enter a store intentionally with a live tag or label to set your system off. They may say something like "oh, this happens to me all the time". That way when they leave and set the Sensormatic system off you will simply allow them to go. Use this as a customer service opportunity to "fix" the customer's problem. A real customer will be appreciative.

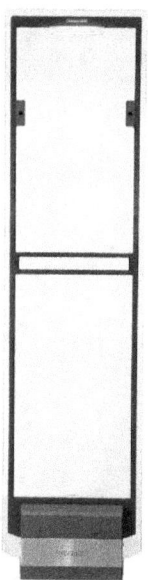

Protect Your Store!

CHAPTER 14

STOPPING AND APPREHENDING A SHOPLIFTER

Okay, you have done everything you can to prevent the losses, but some knucklehead still goes for it. What do you do? First, you need to ensure that you follow any and all local and state laws. There is some variance from state to state, so I will keep this part at a higher level.

You have customer serviced them to death, but you still suspect that they have concealed merchandise.

The Laws governing shoplifting apprehension and arrest generally favor the merchant. However, employees must understand the law and its limits.

In my way of thinking, only management should apprehend a suspect. The following details should occur before a suspect is detained:

YOU MUST SEE the customer remove the merchandise and conceal it.

YOU MUST KNOW what the merchandise is and where the shoplifter concealed it.

YOU MUST NOT LOSE SIGHT of the shoplifter, even for a short period of time.

YOU MUST SEE the shoplifter leaving the store, having gone past the POS or the front doors depending on the layout of your store, without paying for the merchandise. As the shoplifter begins to pass what you consider to be the point of no return, you should make your approach. Some states allow for apprehension as soon as the shoplifter conceals the merchandise.

EXCEPTION: Obvious theft; when the shoplifter takes a large quantity of merchandise without concealing it and runs toward the door.

Remember that you can never take another person's word that they saw someone steal. If you did not see the theft occur, you must assume that it did not happen.

WHEN IN DOUBT-DON'T DETAIN!

When approaching a shoplifter, be sure to be firm, and positive. Address the shoplifter politely and directly. Identify yourself and immediately attempt to recover the merchandise. If possible, another employee should  accompany you when the approach is made.

Note the description of the shoplifter. Pay special attention to height, general build, color of hair and eyes, and noticeable facial or physical characteristics as well as type and color of clothing. In the event the shoplifter runs away, this information will become very important.

Observe any vehicles the shoplifter uses to flee the area. Note the color and type of vehicle and the license tag number.

When the shoplifter surrenders the merchandise, firmly and politely ask that he/she accompany you to the store's office area.

Notify the police that you have a shoplifter in custody. Request that an officer respond.

Shoplifters must not be left alone. For obvious reasons, when female suspects are apprehended, a female store employee must continuously be present while the shoplifter is detained.

While holding shoplifters for the police, limit conversation to simple assurances that they will be treated fairly. The shoplifter should not be ridiculed, intimidated, physically or verbally abused in any way.

If shoplifters ignore attempts to detain them and leave the store, immediately telephone the police to report the event. I do not recommend that you use force.

Describe the physical appearance of the shoplifter.
Describe any vehicles used and the direction of travel.

Do not chase or attempt to follow suspected shoplifters if they leave the store. Once you leave your store, you also leave behind the protection it provides. You leave behind witnesses, phone support, physical support and more.

Most shoplifters are not violent. However, there is always the possibility that the shoplifter could become abusive, hostile or violent toward you. If this happens, keep calm, stay alert, and get away from the person. Immediately notify the police about the incident. Remember, nothing in our store is worth your safety, the safety of our customers, or the safety of your fellow employees.

Complete an internal incident report. This is very important. If, and when this case goes to court, you will not remember details that are important. Write them down, NOW!

You can easily check the shoplifting laws for your state by going to your secretary of state's web site and searching for shoplifting and merchant laws.

Shoplifting apprehensions should be a last resort. If you have a layered approach to your shoplifting problem, then apprehensions should be few and far between. Aggressive customer service and a Sensormatic system will stop most of these losses.

Is there a value to us, as retailers, to make a shoplifter apprehension? In my opinion, yes! But there are dangers when stopping a shoplifter. A shoplifter could become violent and harm you, your staff, and your customers. However, most shoplifters are non-violent. Treat them with professional respect. If you do not take a stand, then shoplifting predators will sense a weakness and continue to attack your store.

Develop your policies and procedures, and train your staff to ensure that those policies and procedures are understood. Follow the policies and procedures and make adjustments as needed. If a shoplifter becomes aggressive, it is best to get the police in route as quickly as possible.

But, should a shoplifter endanger anyone, it is best to allow them to escape. It is not worth anyone's injuries over a piece of merchandise. Keep in mind that you may have lost that battle but you are winning the war. The shoplifter who runs off knows you have caught them and will probably not return to the store. Document the incident, call the police and file a report. If they do come back, call the police immediately. Once the officers arrive, let them know what has happened in the past and ask them to remove the person. At that time, you should "tresspass" the person from your store(s).

CHAPTER 15

CONTACTING THE POLICE

When you call the police, you need to keep in mind that police officers have a wide range of "customers". They provide protection to entire communities. From patrolling neighborhoods, directing traffic and investigating crimes, police officers' jobs are difficult. But overall, they do a great job.

I personally feel that we need twice as many police officers than what we have now, but that is a tax and budget issue. I was a police officer for several years, and have nothing but the utmost respect for what they do and how well they do it!

For a police officer to do his/her job well, they need to prioritize. A robbery in progress' call gets higher priority than Mrs. Jones' cat stuck in a tree. It is a good and generally logical system. But, it can be frustrating to many of us when we hear that an officer will not be with us shortly.

I strongly believe that you should call the police on every shoplifter. There is a strategy that you can use to help yourself do this. It starts before you ever stop a single shoplifter. You need to make contact with your police department. This can start with calling the non-emergency line (not 911), and ask for the supervisor (sergeant or Lt.) over your area. Ask him/her if they would come out to your store and look at your operation. Ask them for their opinion about properly securing your store. Are there any issues in your area that you should watch for? What can you do to assist them in crime prevention? And so on.

I remember when I bought my first office property. I went to the quarterly zone meeting for my area. The police commander presented an excellent PowerPoint presentation about issues and crime in the zone. Then he said, "Now about the prostitution problem at the corner of XX". OMG, that was the intersection where my office building was. I had no idea that issue was occurring near there. I approached him after the meeting and we discussed it. He was actually happy to meet me and discuss it.

As the months went by, we assisted the police department fixing the problem. We even allowed them to use our building to do some surveillance to gather information. Working together, we assisted the police department in solving a problem in our community.

Okay, my employees had some fun with all of this too. Which is okay with me. How many times do you actually get to be involved with something that could be a good episode of COPS?

Because of the prostitution situation, we developed a relationship with the police department that endured even to this day.

When officers were responding to a call we made because of a problem, they were responding to faces and people they knew and trusted rather than simply a faceless address.

Forge a relationship with the police department in your area. Make sure they are always welcome to be in your parking lot. And if they need a warm, quiet place to do their reports, they know they are welcome in your store. An offered cup of coffee never hurts either! Our police officers are special and highly trained individuals that are never appreciated as much as they deserve. A kind word, and even the offer of a cup of coffee means a lot to the folks that protect us every day.

When you do have to call them, make sure you give them the information they need. Briefly describe the situation at hand.

For example, "This is Bill Bregar at Loss Prevention Systems, 123 Main

St., phone number, 123-456-7890, we have apprehended a shoplifter who has stolen merchandise. We need an officer to respond".

The dispatcher will take this information, ask you several questions, and let you know the response time. Remember, this entire call is always recorded. Now, it is the time to also mention, whether the shoplifter is being difficult, abusive, verbal, or physical. This could change the priority of your call. But, a note of caution here; do not cry wolf. If the shoplifter is being cooperative and relatively calm, do not state otherwise.

But if you truly feel that you, your staff or customers are in danger, let the dispatcher know. It may be tempting to do this every time , but believe me when I tell you that you will only get away with that once or twice. After that, in the police officer's eyes you are really part of the problem, not the solution.

When the officer arrives on the scene, explain what you saw and did. The officer will also pull the shoplifter to the side and ask him/her some questions. That is normal and routine. Remember, the officer's job is to make a preliminary decision. If a crime has occurred the officer will take action. In my opinion, you should never demand that the shoplifter be arrested. Let the officer make that decision on his/her own. Keep in mind that if the shoplifter is arrested and charged, it will be by "The State of (your State) vs. Bob the Shoplifter". The government is prosecuting the case, not you. The officer may or may not place the shoplifter in custody or hand cuffs. That is the officer's decision to make. In some cases, they may write them a form of a "ticket".

There is something else you should do at this time. In the officer's presence, you should inform the shoplifter that he/she is trespassed from your property. They are never to return again, ever. Document this in your own records and make a note of the officer's name and badge number. If at a later date, the shoplifter comes into your store, they can be charged with criminal trespass.

In many cases this is a more serious crime than shoplifting. By doing this, word will get around to the shoplifting community that you mean business and to leave you alone.

At this point the shoplifter enters the criminal justice and court systems. You may be required to testify at a hearing or trial.

It is very important that you sit down the very day this incident occurs, and make some notes about what happened. What you did, what the shoplifter said and did, etc. You will find this information invaluable if you have to testify or even just discuss it with the district attorney's office or the court. Writing it down is the only way to be accurate, especially if the case does not come up for a long time. The last thing you want to do is being wishy washy about facts and testimony.

CHAPTER 16

CRIMINAL AND CIVIL COURT

In some cases, the court will ask you (the victim) what you want out of the case. Think about this carefully. We would love to see this horrible person who thought nothing about stealing out of your pocket, to be locked in a room and throw away not just the key but the entire room!

As clogged as the jails and prison facilities are, it is unlikely the judge is going to take precious space for a shoplifter vs a violent criminal. Therefore, your strategy should be different. Your approach should be to get the shoplifter put on the longest probation possible. If the court suggests one year, advocate for two years. A fine is also a good thing to push for. Basically, you want to make the shoplifter's life a living hell for as long as possible. If restitution is ordered, then that money flows through the court so you do not have to play "collection agency". Speaking of restitution, you should ask for as much restitution as possible, even if you recovered all your merchandise and it was still sellable. You should be compensated by the shoplifter for your lost time, wages, loss of sales and inconvenience. Remember, you are the victim here.

Regardless of whether or not this goes to court, or the shoplifter pleas out to a lesser charge, you should be compensated. You should also ask the court to make the criminal trespass a formal part of the record at this point. You will NEVER recover everything from your loss in this incident. But that is not the loss prevention strategy. If you draw this line in the sand, word will get around to not mess with you. That is the ultimate goal here.

Something else that you should do after the incident is settled, is to write a letter to the chief of police or sheriff. It only takes a few minutes, but it lets them know how great a job the officers and detectives did, even if they thought it was just routine. Maybe they could have done a better job in your eyes, but that is not the point.

Remember what I said earlier. These folks get very few complements and many complaints. By sending that letter, you let them know how grateful you are, and that you believe and trust in them. This letter will make it to the officer's personnel file. They mean a great deal when it comes to reviews and promotions.

You may also find that officers will respond to your store's calls promptly, and they will help keep an eye on things. This is not favoritism but simply human nature. The police are good people, doing a tough job they love, but would like to be appreciated for it. In turn, they want to help the people they serve and who like their work product.

You can also pursue a shoplifter in civil court. In the United States, criminal and civil courts are separate. So, while the criminal case is winding its way through the criminal court system, you can file a civil suit, action, or demand against the shoplifter. The criminal and civil courts systems have different rules and procedures. In order to win in a criminal court, we must meet the standard of "guilt beyond a reasonable doubt". In other words, when reasonable people (judge or jury) consider the case, they believe that the bad guy is guilty. In a civil court, we must get a "preponderance of evidence". That means that the scales of justice need to tip 51% in our favor.

If we obtain guilt beyond a reasonable doubt in a criminal case, then the lesser standard of a preponderance of evidence would be met. We do not have to sue someone to get restitution.

You or your attorney, in accordance with your state's laws, can send a demand letter for restitution threatening to sue if the shoplifter doesn't pay up. This can be done in addition to any judgment in criminal court. However, before you run out and think that this is a gold mine to recover your losses, keep in mind that many of these shoplifters have no assets worth taking.

I would not recommend that path to be your goal. Although, if you do recover funds, that is awesome. The real value you get here is the message you send to the shoplifting community. That word does get around.

What I like about pursuing both civil and criminal options, is that it makes the shoplifter's life a living hell. Even for someone who has no assets. If it is a juvenile, then you go after the parents. In many cases, parents will settle or pay for your losses and expenses to resolve the issue.

A special note about juveniles and parents. When I file criminal charges against a juvenile and the parents contact us, they do so in one of two ways.

First, it's the confrontational and angry response. "My Johnny would never do something like that, I am going to sue." Or, we see a more adult approach where you clearly see that they are concerned about what their child did, and that the child may be on the wrong path.

When I am approached by people in the angry, threatening mode, I do not discuss anything with them. Many times, these people feel that if they threaten you with a lawsuit, that you will back down. Their problem-solving skills are not very developed, and thus they resort to that approach. I simply refer them to the attorney and do not discuss anything with them.

However, if I see true concern for their child and the parents are truly trying to fix the child's behavior, then I have a tendency to try to work with them. Children make mistakes, 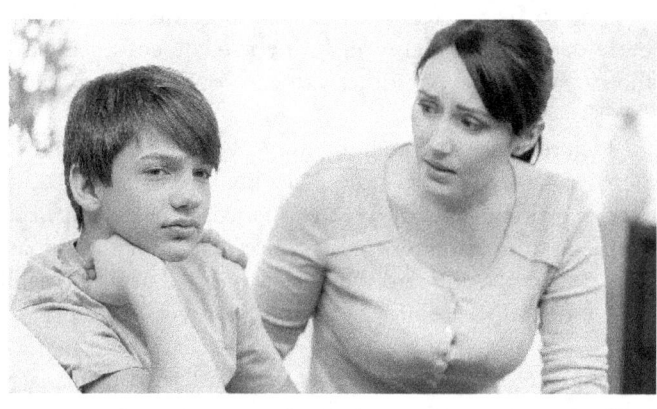 which is part of what being a child is all about. That is also why the laws in our country put them in a special category. But, the key here is that if the parents want to truly fix the problem, there have to be consequences for the child to learn from. For a first offense, they get community service and/or court supervised probation that drops from their record once completed. Restitution to the retailer has to be made as well.

There are companies that specialize in civil recovery from both shoplifters and employees who steal. I have used them in the past when I was a loss prevention manager or director for previous companies. I have also used a private attorney.

When I was director of loss prevention for the athlete's foot (think Nike, Reebok...) I utilized the services of an Atlanta attorney, Susan Murphey. She now owns her own firm, Murphey's Law. The name of the firm is funny when you add their tag line, "Anything that CAN go wrong WILL go wrong."

Susan is rather aggressive when it comes to recovery in these situations. She developed a national program for us that really paid dividends, in both recovery dollars and setting the standard that you do not steal from the company. If you want to discuss your civil and criminal options, you can reach Susan at www.MurpheysLawFirm.com.

We should also discuss the civil and criminal pursuit of juveniles, the elderly and special needs folks. In some cases, you will call the police and the officer who arrives at your store will try to talk you out of any action. This generally happens because handling one of these folks is more burdensome for the officer, than others. That should not influence your judgment. In fact, shame on any police officer who does this. It does nothing to fix the real problem just because they do not want to do a bit more paperwork. You want to involve law enforcement when someone in this category is caught, otherwise you could incur trouble.

Picture this; you catch any one of these people but let them go with a stern warning. Let's say the child then goes home and tells his parents a very one-sided story of what happened. You do not need to deal with the problems this brings. Let the police deal with this situation. That is what they do for a living and they are very good at it. Remember, in a criminal case, it is "The State of XX. Vs Johnny Juvenile Shoplifter".

The same applies to the elderly and special needs folks. The district attorney may ask you down the road to consider other options. That is great and worth discussing because again, you are trying to send a message. That is also accomplishing your goal.

CHAPTER 17

IT IS ALL IMPORTANT

In a retailer's effort to prevent shoplifting, we must never forget our good customers. These are the people that pay the bills. The good news is that, in our effort to prevent shoplifting and our quest for sales from our good customers, the solutions are the same.

Customer service is a key factor to increase sales. We know that the more attention we pay to our customers, the more sales will increase.

A well-staffed store with highly trained employees, makes a customer feel special and comfortable in a shopping environment.

One of the advantages that a small retailer has over the big discount stores such as Walmart, or Target, is that customer service is readily available on the sales floor. Have you ever tried to get help at one of the big stores? You can wander the store aimlessly looking for someone, without finding the help you need. You may even have to return to the front of the store for help, which can be a hike.

Shoplifters on the other hand, hate customer service. They want to be anonymous and blend into the background.

So, when you provide them with even a small amount of customer service, you drive them crazy and prevent shoplifting. Why? Because a shoplifter needs some privacy, even for a few moments, to steal. You take that option away when you offer them great customer service . This is especially true if you check back on them, linger or work in the area.

I have seen many shoplifters get frustrated and simply leave the store when we provide good customer service. The only problem with this concept is that, as we have tighter labor budgets we have less customer service support on the sales floor. To counter this, you have to either accept higher shoplifting losses, or put tools in place such as a Sensormatic system. These tools can extend your customer service reach. Sensormatic systems change the shoplifting dynamic in the store. Even if there is a high customer to employee ratio, the shoplifter is much more uncomfortable and tends to simply go elsewhere.

Using customer service is not just a tool for increased sales, it is a weapon in the war to prevent shoplifting.

To get the most value out of this book, I suggest you get started today improving customer service and having frequent meetings with your employees about these topics.

As I mentioned, email me at bbregar@losspreventionsystems.com or call me at 1-866-914-2567 and request a free copy of the customizable shoplifting policy and procedure template you can use to craft your own store policy.

You can also learn a great deal about all of these topics by signing up for our newsletter at www.LossPreventionSystems.com

The information contained in this book is general in nature and intended solely for informational and educational purposes. Nothing contained herein or presented is intended to be nor should it be construed to be legal advice. Every situation is different. Consult a legal or loss prevention specialist for specific advice concerning your situation.

RESOURCES

Loss Prevention technology and techniques are changing all the time. To keep updated, here are some resources you can visit.

www.LossPreventionSystems.com - Make sure to sign up for the email updates to keep up to date.

www.RetailLossPreventionStore.com - Once you sign up for the store, you can see all pricing. If you have a question also give us a call.

www.PreventShopliftingLoss.net - Read our monthly magazine on shoplifting prevention.

www.Facebook.com/LossPreventionSystems is our Facebook page with lots of updates and videos - stop by and let us know how you liked the book.

www.youtube.com/c/LossPreventionSystems is our library of videos about shoplifting topics and highlighting shoplifting prevention products.

And remember, Bill wants to talk to you if you are a small to midsized retailer looking to boost profits by cutting down loss. Call 1-866-914-2567 or email Bill at bbregar@losspreventionsystems.com to schedule a time to review your needs.

HIRE BILL BREGAR TO SPEAK

Bill Bregar is your Loss Prevention Speaker. Are you looking for a loss prevention professional to speak at your next company conference, group or association meeting?

Bill is an accomplished, high energy speaker who will deliver a presentation on loss prevention topics including employee theft, shoplifting, and an LP approach to hiring, understanding the employee that steals and more, anywhere in the US.

Bill started his career in LP and Security over 30 years ago and has been the Director of Loss Prevention for several major companies. Bill draws on his experience in LP experience including the thousands of employee theft investigations he has conducted. He has put in place anti-shoplifting programs that have led to significant reductions in loss and an increase in profit for many companies.

Bill has a Bachelor's degree in Private Security Administration and Management.

Speaking engagements, seminars or training can be from one hour up to several days; each presentation is customized to your needs.

Let's discuss your loss prevention speaker needs. Give Bill a call at 1-866-914-2567.

BULK BOOK PURCHASES

This book is a must read for managers, assistant managers and key employees. Having one at each POS can improve training and top of mind awareness in your store employees as well.

If you wish to order books directly from Loss Prevention Systems for a 25% discount on 3 or more books, call 1-866-914-2567.

Buy 25 books or more and get a live virtual training session with the author at no additional charge. Call for details.

www.ingramcontent.com/pod-product-compliance
Lightning Source LLC
Chambersburg PA
CBHW071219220526
45468CB00002B/671